WealthWise Women:
Releasing a Financial Feminist
Era

Robert Y. Smith

ABOUT THE AUTHOR

Robert Y. Smith is a passionate advocate for financial equality and empowerment. With a background in finance and a deep commitment to social justice, he has dedicated his career to promoting financial literacy, advocating for gender-inclusive policies, and fostering entrepreneurship among women.

As the author of "Wealth Wise Women," Smith brings a unique perspective to the conversation surrounding gender-based financial disparities. His expertise in finance, combined with his understanding of the systemic barriers that hinder women's economic empowerment, allows him to offer practical insights and actionable strategies for achieving financial equality.

Smith's work is not limited to the pages of his book; he is actively involved in community initiatives and advocacy efforts aimed at promoting financial inclusivity. Through workshops, speaking engagements, and collaborations with organizations, he continues to champion the cause of financial feminism, inspiring individuals and institutions to take meaningful steps towards a more equitable financial landscape.

As a thought leader and advocate, Robert Y. Smith is committed to creating a future where financial equality is not just a dream but a reality for all. His dedication to this cause shines through in "Wealth Wise Women," a book that serves as both a call to action and a roadmap for achieving economic empowerment for women.

CHAPTER 1.. 6
CHAPTER 2.. 9
CHAPTER 3.. 12
CHAPTER 4.. 16
CHAPTER 5.. 20
CHAPTER 6.. 26
CONCLUSION...29

INTRODUCTION

Definition of financial feminist

Financial women's rights arise as a crucial power inside the more extensive range of orientation uniformity, supporting ladies' financial strengthening. This development tries to destroy settlements in structures that propagate monetary differences, recognizing the significant effect these awkward natures have on the general prosperity and independence of ladies. At its substance, monetary women's liberation fills in as an impetus for changing cultural standards and frameworks to encourage a more even-handed monetary scene.

Characterized by a guarantee to correct foundational imbalances, monetary women's rights dig into the complex difficulties faced by ladies in the domains of pay, abundance gathering, and venture valuable open doors. It

goes past tending to simple compensation holes, including an extensive assessment of the
fundamental factors that add to irregular monetary characteristics.

One of the focal precepts of monetary women's rights is the acknowledgment that monetary education is an integral asset for strengthening. Through schooling and mindfulness, the development looks to close the information hole that frequently leaves ladies in a difficult spot in exploring complex monetary scenes. By furnishing ladies with the abilities and information fundamental for informed direction, monetary women's rights plans to engage them to assume responsibility for their financial predeterminations.

Additionally, monetary women's liberation advocates for working environment strengthening, requesting equivalent open doors, advancements, and fair pay. It challenges imbued predispositions and biased rehearsals that block ladies' advancement in proficient circles. This part of the development isn't simply a call for equity but an essential move to reshape corporate societies and designs, encouraging conditions that are worth and prize the commitments, everything being equal, paying little heed to orientation.

As monetary women's rights pick up speed, it broadens its venture into the domain of speculation systems, encouraging ladies to defeat verifiable obstructions and effectively take part in establishing financial stability and valuable open doors. By tending to take a chance with insights and empowering vital speculation, the development tries to make everything fair and scaffold the venture hole that has long been burdened.

CHAPTER 1

Financial Disparities

In the complex embroidery of our monetary scene, obvious disparities persevere, influencing the monetary prosperity of people in light of their orientation. This part digs into the multi-layered domain of monetary inconsistencies, uncovering the nuanced layers of the orientation pay hole, abundance aggregation contrasts, and venture holes that shape the monetary stories of people.

1: The Orientation Pay Hole

The orientation pay hole, a determined and petulant issue, creates a shaded area over proficient domains. Investigate the foundations of this uniqueness, inspecting elements like word-related isolation, exchange elements, and cultural assumptions. Divulge the genuine degree of the pay differential and its suggestions for ladies' monetary strengthening.

2: Abundance Aggregation Contrasts

While pay is one perspective, abundance incorporates a more extensive range of monetary prosperity. Examine how orientation-based disparities in legacy, property proprietorship, and admittance to monetary assets add to disparate abundance aggregation. Shed light on the intensifying impacts that prevent ladies' monetary strength and long-haul security.

3: Speculation Holes

Dive into the complexities of speculation differences, investigating how ladies experience exceptional difficulties entering and flourishing in the venture scene. Reveal the effect of hazard insight, admittance to monetary schooling, and speculation valuable open doors on molding different monetary directions for people.

As we set out on this investigation of monetary incongruities, the focal point will zero in on the actual differences and the hidden designs and predispositions that sustain them. By understanding the foundations of these inconsistencies, we prepare for the network.

CHAPTER 2

Empowering through Education

Schooling remains an impressive power in destroying the hindrances that sustain monetary variations. This part unwinds the essential job of training in cultivating monetary fairness, underscoring the significance of monetary proficiency for ladies and the basics of shutting the information hole.

1: Monetary Proficiency for Ladies

Connecting the Data Gap
Research the basic significance of monetary proficiency customized to the special necessities and difficulties faced by ladies. Investigate drives and projects that furnish ladies with the information and abilities important to explore the intricacies of

individual budgets, speculations, and abundance of the board.

2: Shutting the Information Hole

Forming Comprehensive Learning Conditions
Dig into the methodologies and ways to deal with closing the information hole that obstructs ladies from completely taking part in monetary navigation. Look at the job of instructive organizations, working environments, and local area programs in establishing comprehensive learning conditions that engage ladies with the devices to pursue informed monetary decisions.

3: Past Nuts and Bolts

High-level Monetary Schooling
Move past essential monetary proficiency to investigate high-level training potential to open doors for ladies. Examine how specific preparation, mentorship programs, and

systems administration open doors to enabling ladies to take on positions of authority in money and business ventures.

By getting it and tending to the instructive parts of monetary aberrations, we not only engage ladies with the information to explore their monetary excursions but additionally lay the basis for foundational change. As we investigate the convergence of training and monetary women's rights, we divulge a way toward a more comprehensive and even-handed monetary scene where ladies are educated as well as enabled to shape their monetary fates.

CHAPTER 3

Workplace Empowerment

Chasing monetary women's liberation, the work
the environment fills in as a critical milestone where equivalent open doors, advancements, and fair pay are goals and basic privileges. This section unwinds the elements of work environment strengthening, revealing insight into the significance of establishing conditions that cultivate proficient development, advocate for fair remuneration, and eventually destroy orientation-based boundaries.

1: Equivalent Open Doors and Advancements

Breaking the Biased impediment
Investigate the verifiable setting of gendered working environment orders and dig into the

elements that add to the carelessness of the unattainable rank. Research fruitful techniques and drives that challenge generalizations, address predispositions and prepare for equivalent open doors and advancements for ladies in different enterprises.

Mentorship and Sponsorship
Look at the job of mentorship and sponsorship programs in driving ladies into positions of authority. Uncover the effect of steady proficient connections in exploring work environment challenges, building certainty, and working with professional success.

2: Support for Fair Remuneration

Shutting the Pay Hole
Explore the complexities of supporting fair remuneration, taking apart the pay hole, and understanding the foundational issues that add to inconsistent compensation. Investigate

the job of exchange abilities, straightforwardness, and authoritative strategies in restricting the remuneration split among people.

Pay Value Drives

Feature effective compensation value drives and approaches that associations can carry out to guarantee decency in pay. Dissect the effect of pay straightforwardness, execution assessments, and legitimacy-based frameworks in encouraging an impartial compensation structure inside work environments.

As we navigate the scene of working environment strengthening, it becomes obvious that making a comprehensive, steady, and fair workplace isn't simply an ethical objective yet in addition an upper hand. By destroying hindrances to approaching open doors and supporting fair remuneration, associations contribute not exclusively to the strengthening of ladies but additionally to the general achievement and supportability of their labor force.

CHAPTER 4

Investment Strategies
Pursuing financial Ladies' freedom, the way
to monetary reinforcing habitually twists
through the location of hypotheses. This part
explores the frameworks and examinations
for women in making monetary prosperity
through adventures, underlining the meaning
of informed bearing, various portfolios, and
long-stretch money-related planning.

1: Adventure Procedures for Financial Turn of Events

Expanding and Informed Autonomous
heading
Uncover the power of upgrade in hypothesis
portfolios and the work it plays in easing
possibilities. Examine adventure systems
redid to the momentous goals and chance
profiles of women, focusing on the meaning

of educated elements in investigating the complexities regarding financial business areas

2: Undertaking and Overflow Creation

The Ambitious Backwoods
Dive into the gig of undertaking as a pathway for women to make wealth. Explore the troubles and entryways looked at by female business visionaries, and examine how money-related ladies' extremist guidelines can be applied to energize advancement, sensibility, and progress in endeavors.

3: Long-stretch Financial Readiness

Getting Financial Destinies
Break down the significance of long-stretch money-related readiness in making and safeguarding monetary energy. Look at retirement orchestrating, estate the board, and the formation of generational abundance as vital parts of an extensive monetary system

that enables ladies to accomplish enduring monetary security.

4: Tending to Take a Chance with Discernments

While creating financial well-being through speculations is significant, the excursion isn't without seeing a chance that might upset monetary strengthening. This section investigates the nuanced scene of chance insights, tending to the mental and cultural elements that influence how ladies approach monetary choices.

- **Unwinding Hazard Discernment Predispositions**

Mental Variables in Navigation

Analyze the mental predispositions that impact risk insight, like misfortune repugnance, and arrogance. Investigate how understanding these inclinations can enable ladies to pursue more sane and key monetary choices lined up with their objectives.

- **Social and Cultural Impacts**

Exploring Outside Tensions

Examine the effect of cultural assumptions, social standards, and orientation generalizations on ladies' gamble discernments. Feature techniques to explore outside pressures, challenge restricting convictions, and develop a mentality that embraces reasonable courses of action for monetary development.

By tending to take a chance with discernment and giving direction on creating financial well-being through ventures, this part expects to outfit ladies with the information and certainty expected to explore the monetary scene, challenge predispositions, and effectively shape their monetary predeterminations.

CHAPTER 5

Entrepreneurship and Financial Independence

Business ventures remain a strong road for ladies to produce their way toward monetary freedom. This section investigates the extraordinary capability of business ventures, giving bits of knowledge into the difficulties and valuable open doors ladies experience as they embark on making and dealing with their organizations.

1: Engaging Ladies Business visionaries

Conquering Difficulties
Analyze the novel difficulties faced by ladies' business people, including admittance to financing, orientation predispositions, and adjusting work-life obligations. Feature examples of overcoming adversity and systems for defeating deterrents, cultivating

versatility, and building flourishing organization

2: Business as an Impetus for Monetary Freedom

Abundance of Creation and Independence
Investigate how business can be an impetus for abundance creation and monetary independence. Break down the effect of ladies-claimed organizations on monetary biological systems and the job of monetary women's activist standards in forming enterprising undertakings that add to individual and aggregate monetary strengthening.

3: Ladies Drove Organizations

Jump into the universe of ladies-driven organizations, investigating the effect of female administration on hierarchical culture, development, and productivity. This section reveals insight into the exceptional characteristics that ladies bring to business initiatives and how these characteristics add to the achievement and manageability of venture

- **Authority Styles and Authoritative Culture**

Encouraging Comprehensive Administration Look at the authority styles regularly found in ladies-driven organizations and their effect on making comprehensive and steady hierarchical societies. Investigate how variety at the top converts into stronger, innovative, and socially mindful organizations.

- **Breaking Obstructions and Reclassifying Achievement**

Feature contextual analyses of ladies who have broken unfair limitations in different ventures, exhibiting the variety of ladies-driven organizations and their aggregate effect on testing conventional standards and reclassifying achievement.

4: Methodologies for Monetary Independence

This part digs into functional techniques ladies can execute to accomplish monetary independence. From planning and saving to key professional arranging, investigate significant advances that engage ladies to assume command over their monetary fates.

• Planning and Monetary Preparation
Defining Monetary Objectives
Guide perusers through the method involved with defining sensible and attainable monetary objectives. Talk about the significance of planning, crisis reserves, and long-haul monetary preparation as basic components for monetary independence.

• Discussion Abilities and Professional Success
Exploring Proficient Directions
Analyze techniques for haggling fair remuneration, looking for advancements, and

progressing in vocations. Feature the meaning of mentorship, organizing, and ceaseless ability advancement in improving monetary independence.

5: Monetary Women's liberation in real life

Unite the key standards examined throughout the book to show how monetary women's liberation can be applied, in actuality, situations. Exhibit motivating instances of ladies who have embraced monetary women's activist standards and taken huge steps toward financial strengthening.

- ## Grassroots Development and Local Area Strengthening

Cooperative Drives

Investigate the effect of grassroots developments and local area-based drives in advancing monetary women's liberation. Feature how to aggregate activity and encourage groups of people to add to destroying foundational obstructions and cultivating financial inclusivity.

- **Backing and Strategy Change**

Molding What's in store

Look at the job of promotion and strategy change in progressing monetary women's liberation on more extensive scale feature instances of regulative changes and drives that advance orientation equity in monetary frameworks and work environments.

By investigating business, ladies-driven organizations, and methodologies for monetary independence, this book expects to furnish ladies with the information and motivation expected to explore their monetary excursions, challenge cultural standards, and effectively shape a more comprehensive and impartial monetary scene.

CHAPTER 6

Government and Policy

In the domain of monetary women's liberation, the impact of government and strategy couldn't possibly be more significant. This section investigates the significant job of support for orientation comprehensive approaches and the need for legitimate changes to destroy obstructions and cultivate monetary balance.

1: Promotion of Orientation Comprehensive Approaches

Forming a Comprehensive Monetary Scene

Look at the significance of supporting orientation comprehensive strategies in molding a more impartial monetary scene. Plunge into the crossing point of government drives and monetary women's activist standards, investigating how arrangements can address foundational inclinations, advance equivalent open doors, and cultivate financial inclusivity.

Work environment Arrangements

Investigate the effect of work environment strategies on orientation balance, including parental leave, adaptable work courses of action, and drives advancing variety and incorporation. Feature contextual investigations of organizations that have effectively executed orientation comprehensive strategies, prompting a more steady and fair workplace.

2: Legitimate Changes for Monetary Correspondence

Tending to Legitimate Hindrances

Reveal the legitimate boundaries that add to monetary imbalance and investigate the requirement for complete lawful changes. Examine biased rehearsals, legacy regulations, and other legitimate systems that lopsidedly influence ladies' monetary prosperity and support for changes to guarantee decency and correspondence.

Monetary Schooling Orders

Analyze the potential for legitimate orders around monetary schooling, guaranteeing that instructive establishments and working environments are expected to give exhaustive monetary proficiency programs that address the remarkable necessities of ladies. Examine how such commands can add to restricting the monetary information hole and cultivating strengthening.

By examining and pushing for the orientation of comprehensive arrangements and lawful changes, this section expects to reveal insight into the groundbreaking capability of government activity in destroying foundational obstructions. Through essential support and lawful changes, we can draw nearer to a future where monetary equity isn't simply a desire but an unmistakable reality for ladies in all features of life.

CONCLUSION

In the excursion through the pages of "Wealth Wise Women," we have explored the unpredictable scene of orientation-based monetary aberrations and dug into the domains of training, work environment strengthening, business, government approaches, and lawful changes. As we conclude this investigation, let us think about the central issues that have enlightened the way toward monetary inclusivity.

Summing up Central issues

- **Figuring out Aberration:** We started by disentangling the complex layers of monetary variations, analyzing the orientation pay hole, abundance gathering contrasts, and venture holes that persevere in our financial frameworks.

- **Engaging Through Training:** Perceiving the extraordinary capability of instruction, we investigated the significance of monetary proficiency for ladies, shutting the information hole, and establishing comprehensive learning conditions that furnish ladies with the apparatuses for monetary direction.

- **WorkingEnvironment Strengthening:** In the working environment, we dug into the meaning of equivalent open doors, advancements, fair pay, and the significant job of authority in ladies-driven organizations. We perceived the working environment as a site of work as well as a stage for promotion and change.

- **Creating Financial Stability and Tending to Dangers:** Directing our concentration toward ventures, business, and chance insights, we revealed procedures for creating financial well-being, exploring pioneering attempts, and tending to mental and cultural variables that impact risk discernments.

- **Government and Strategy Support**: Recognizing the impact of government and strategy, we investigated the promotion of orientation comprehensive strategies and lawful changes that can destroy foundational hindrances and encourage monetary uniformity on a more extensive scale.

Source of Inspiration for Monetary Inclusivity

As we close this excursion, it is fundamental to perceive that accomplishing monetary inclusivity requires aggregate exertion and support responsibility. The source of inspiration is clear:

- **Advance Monetary Instruction:** Backer for complete monetary training programs that are comprehensive, available, and customized to the assorted requirements of ladies. Support drives that span the information hole and enable ladies to pursue informed monetary choices.

- **Champion Work environment Correspondence**: Take part in discussions and drives that challenge work environment predispositions, advance equivalent open doors, and support for fair remuneration. Support ladies' administration and business ventures in the working environment, cultivating conditions that energize development and coordinated effort.

- **Put resources into Ladies:** Whether through business ventures, speculation systems, or monetary preparation, effectively put resources into ladies' prosperity. Support ladies claimed organizations, mentorship projects, and drives that advance financial strengthening.

- **Advocate for Strategy Change:** Speak more loudly to support orientation comprehensive arrangements and lawful changes. Team up with associations and policymakers to address fundamental hindrances and add to the production of a more even-handed monetary scene.

In the crossing point of monetary women's rights and the source of inspiration for monetary inclusivity, we track down the ability to reshape our financial accounts. By working on the whole to destroy obstructions, challenge standards, and engage ladies at each level, we prepare for a future where monetary equity isn't simply an objective but a reality for all. The excursion towards monetary inclusivity is progressing, and every one of us plays a crucial part in forming an additional fair and enabled world.

www.ingramcontent.com/pod-product-compliance
Lightning Source LLC
Chambersburg PA
CBHW072259310526
45795CB00012B/1853